No Time to Cook™

One-Dish Meals

READY TO SERVE IN 30 MINUTES OR LESS

Publications International, Ltd.

No Time to Cook is a trademark of Publications International, Ltd.

Pictured on the front cover: Four-Cheese Stuffed Shells *(page 82)*.

Pictured on the back cover: Gazebo Chicken *(page 44)*.

ISBN: 0-7853-1979-4

Manufactured in U.S.A.

8   7   6   5   4   3   2   1

Nutritional Analysis: In the case of multiple choices, the first ingredient, the lowest amount and the lowest serving yield are used to calculate the nutritional analysis. "Serve with" suggestions are not included unless otherwise stated.

Microwave Cooking: Microwave ovens vary in wattage. The microwave cooking times given in this publication are approximate. Use the cooking times as guidelines and check for doneness before adding more time. Consult manufacturer's instructions for suitable microwave-safe cooking dishes.

No Time to Cook™

One-Dish Meals

CONTENTS

WHAT'S YOUR SPEED, WHAT'S YOUR NEED?

The recipes in this publication are divided into four categories. These classifications, noted under the title of each recipe, are as follows:

PANTRY COOKING

The ultimate convenience: No-Stop Shopping! Whip up these delicious recipes in 30 minutes or less with ingredients already on hand in your kitchen.

20 MINUTES OR LESS

Great taste in no time! These fuss-free dishes are a snap to prepare in 20 minutes or less with a little help from convenience foods.

6 INGREDIENTS OR LESS

See just how much flavor can come from so few ingredients (not including salt, pepper or water)! Ready to serve in 30 minutes or less, these simple recipes will keep your shopping time and your cooking time to a minimum.

MAKE–AHEAD RECIPE

Prepare these mouthwatering dishes when you have the time . . . then enjoy them even more when you don't! Cook according to your schedule—hours, days or even several weeks ahead of time—so a fresh, homemade dish can still be savored on those extra-busy days.

WHAT'S THE TIME?

Each recipe includes a "prep and cook" time. These times are based on the approximate amount of time needed to assemble and prepare ingredients prior to cooking and the minimum amount of time required to cook, broil, microwave or chill the foods in the recipe. These recipes have been developed for the most efficient use of your time. Some preparation steps are completed before the cooking begins, while others are done during the cooking time.

S E N S E

One-dish meals are every cook's idea of a casual, effortless meal. From light soups and salads to filling casseroles and skillet dishes, one-dish meals are quick to fix and easy to clean up. They can be served alone or with simple accompaniments, such as fresh fruit, raw vegetables or hot bread. With this selection of delicious recipes, you'll be in and out of the kitchen in a flash.

PANTRY POWER

Discover the power of a well-stocked pantry. Keep the following items on hand for spur-of-the-moment stir-fries:

- ✔ a variety of bottled sauces, such as stir-fry sauce, teriyaki marinade, plum sauce, sweet-and-sour sauce and peanut sauce

- ✔ bottled chopped garlic and ginger

- ✔ quick-cooking rice

- ✔ a selection of fresh vegetables or frozen Asian-style vegetable blends

- ✔ frozen meat, poultry and seafood, such as boneless chicken breasts, chicken tenders, boneless chicken thighs, boneless pork loin, pork tenderloin, beef sirloin, beef flank steak and shrimp

ALMOST HOMEMADE

Convenience foods can help put fresh-from-the-oven breads on the table in a minimum of time without sacrificing flavor. Try some of these easy ideas:

- Jazz up sweet muffin mixes by adding streusel toppings, chopped nuts, grated citrus peel or fruit pieces.

- Spice up corn muffin or corn bread mixes with chopped canned jalapeño or green chilies, shredded jalapeño Jack cheese, minced onion, chopped pimiento or thawed frozen corn.

- Dress up refrigerated biscuit, crescent roll and bread stick doughs by spraying them with nonstick olive oil cooking spray, dipping them in melted butter or brushing them with beaten egg white before rolling them in crushed dried herbs, grated Parmesan cheese, sesame seeds, poppy seeds or cracked black pepper.

6 INGREDIENTS OR LESS

Stir-Fry Beef & Vegetable Soup

1 pound boneless beef
steak, such as sirloin
or round steak
2 teaspoons Asian
sesame oil, divided
3 cans (about 14 ounces
each) reduced-
sodium beef broth
1 package (16 ounces)
frozen stir-fry
vegetables
3 green onions, thinly
sliced
¼ cup bottled stir-fry
sauce

1 Slice beef across grain into ⅛-inch-thick strips; cut strips into bite-size pieces.

2 Heat Dutch oven over high heat. Add 1 teaspoon oil and tilt pan to coat bottom. Add half the beef in single layer; cook 1 minute, without stirring, until slightly browned on bottom. Turn and brown other side about 1 minute. Remove beef from pan with slotted spoon; set aside. Repeat with remaining 1 teaspoon oil and beef; set aside.

3 Add broth to Dutch oven; cover and bring to a boil over high heat. Add vegetables; reduce heat to medium-high and simmer 3 to 5 minutes or until heated through. Add beef, green onions and stir-fry sauce; simmer 1 minute more. *Makes 6 servings*

Prep and cook time: 22 minutes

Serving suggestion: Make a quick sesame bread to serve with the soup. Brush refrigerated dinner roll dough with water, then dip in sesame seeds before baking.

Nutrients per serving: Calories: 159, Total Fat: 5 g, Protein: 20 g, Carbohydrate: 7 g, Cholesterol: 43 mg, Sodium: 356 mg, Dietary Fiber: trace
Dietary Exchanges: Bread: ½, Meat: 2

Hearty Pasta and Chick-Pea Chowder

6 ounces uncooked rotini pasta
2 tablespoons olive oil
¾ cup chopped onion
½ cup chopped celery
½ cup thinly sliced carrot
2 cloves garlic, minced
¼ cup all-purpose flour
1½ teaspoons Italian seasoning
⅛ teaspoon crushed red pepper flakes
⅛ teaspoon black pepper
2 cans (about 14 ounces each) chicken broth
1 can (19 ounces) chick-peas, drained and rinsed
1 can (14½ ounces) Italian-style stewed tomatoes, undrained
6 slices bacon

1 Cook rotini according to package directions. Rinse, drain and set aside.

2 Meanwhile, heat oil in 4-quart Dutch oven over medium-high heat until hot. Add onion, celery, carrot and garlic. Reduce heat to medium; cook and stir 5 to 6 minutes or until vegetables are crisp-tender.

3 Remove from heat. Stir in flour, Italian seasoning, red pepper and black pepper until well blended. Gradually stir in broth. Return to heat and bring to a boil, stirring frequently. Boil, stirring constantly, 1 minute. Reduce heat to medium. Stir in cooked pasta, chick-peas and tomatoes. Cook 5 minutes or until heated through.

4 Meanwhile, place bacon between double layer of paper towels on paper plate. Microwave on HIGH 5 to 6 minutes or until bacon is crisp. Drain and crumble.

5 Sprinkle each serving with bacon. Serve immediately.
Makes 6 (1-cup) servings

Prep and cook time: 30 minutes

Serving suggestion: Top with grated Parmesan cheese and serve with crusty bread, salad greens tossed with Italian dressing and fruit cobbler.

Nutrients per serving: Calories: 347, Total Fat: 11 g, Protein: 13 g, Carbohydrate: 50 g, Cholesterol: 16 mg, Sodium: 1,168 mg, Dietary Fiber: 6 g
Dietary Exchanges: Vegetable: 2, Bread: 3, Fat: 2

Chicken Stew with Dumplings

2 tablespoons vegetable oil
2 cups sliced carrots
1 cup chopped onion
1 large green bell pepper, sliced
½ cup sliced celery
2 cans (about 14 ounces each) reduced-sodium chicken broth
¼ cup plus 2 tablespoons all-purpose flour
2 pounds boneless skinless chicken breasts, cut into 1-inch pieces
3 medium potatoes, unpeeled and cut into 1-inch pieces
6 ounces mushrooms, halved
¾ cup frozen peas
1½ teaspoons dried basil leaves, divided
1¼ teaspoons dried rosemary, divided
½ teaspoon dried tarragon, divided
¾ to 1 teaspoon salt
¼ teaspoon black pepper
2 cups biscuit mix
⅔ cup 2% milk

1 Heat oil in 4-quart Dutch oven over medium heat until hot. Add carrots, onion, bell pepper and celery; cook and stir 5 minutes or until onion is tender. Stir in chicken broth, reserving ½ cup; bring to a boil. Mix reserved ½ cup broth and flour; stir into boiling mixture. Boil, stirring constantly, 1 minute or until thickened. Stir chicken, potatoes, mushrooms, peas, 1 teaspoon basil, ¾ teaspoon rosemary and ¼ teaspoon tarragon into mixture. Reduce heat to low; simmer, covered, 18 to 20 minutes or until vegetables are almost tender and chicken is no longer pink in center. Add salt and pepper; cool completely. Refrigerate, covered, up to 2 days.

2 To complete recipe, bring stew just to a boil in large saucepan over medium heat. For dumplings, combine biscuit mix, remaining ½ teaspoon basil, ½ teaspoon rosemary and ¼ teaspoon tarragon in small bowl; stir in milk to form soft dough. Spoon dumpling mixture on top of stew in 8 large spoonfuls. Reduce heat to low. Cook, uncovered, 10 minutes. Cover and cook 10 minutes or until biscuits are tender and toothpick inserted in center comes out clean. Serve in shallow bowls.
Makes 8 (1¼-cup) servings

Make-ahead time: up to 2 days before serving
Final prep and cook time: 30 minutes

Nutrients per serving: Calories: 431, Total Fat: 12 g, Protein: 34 g, Carbohydrate: 46 g, Cholesterol: 70 mg, Sodium: 839 mg, Dietary Fiber: 3 g
Dietary Exchanges: Vegetable: 1, Bread: 3, Meat: 3

Tuna Corn Chowder

2 strips bacon
1 small onion
2 ribs celery, chopped
1½ tablespoons all-purpose flour
2 cups 2% milk
½ teaspoon dried thyme leaves
¼ teaspoon salt
¼ teaspoon pepper
1 cup frozen whole kernel corn
1 can (6 ounces) tuna packed in water, drained

1 Cook bacon in medium saucepan over medium-high heat until brown and crisp, turning once. Drain on paper towels, reserving drippings in saucepan.

2 Add onion and celery to pan drippings; cook and stir over medium-high heat 3 minutes or until onion is tender.

3 Add flour, stirring until well blended; cook 1 minute. Stir in milk, thyme, salt and pepper. Cook, stirring frequently, until thickened.

4 Stir in corn and tuna; cook over medium heat 5 minutes or until corn is tender, stirring frequently.

5 Crumble bacon. Serve chowder sprinkled with bacon.
Makes 2 servings

Prep and cook time: 25 minutes

For a special touch, top chowder with red bell pepper strips or popped popcorn.

Nutrients per serving: Calories: 379, Total Fat: 8 g, Protein: 39 g, Carbohydrate: 38 g, Cholesterol: 23 mg, Sodium: 824 mg, Dietary Fiber: 3 g
Dietary Exchanges: Milk: 1, Vegetable: 1, Bread: 1½, Meat: 3

Smoked Sausage Gumbo

¾ pound Polish or other
smoked sausage
1 cup uncooked long-
grain converted
white rice
1 medium onion, diced
1 green bell pepper, diced
2 ribs celery, chopped
1 large carrot, chopped
2 teaspoons dried
oregano leaves
2 teaspoons dried thyme
leaves
⅛ teaspoon ground red
pepper
¼ cup all-purpose flour
2 tablespoons olive oil
1 can (14½ ounces)
diced tomatoes,
undrained
1 can (about 14 ounces)
chicken broth

1 Bring 2 cups water to a boil in medium saucepan over high heat. Meanwhile, cut sausage in half lengthwise, then crosswise into ½-inch slices.

2 Stir rice into boiling water. Reduce heat to low; cover and simmer 18 minutes or until liquid is absorbed.

3 While rice is cooking, place sausage, onion, bell pepper, celery, carrot, oregano, thyme and red pepper in large microwavable container. Cover and cook on HIGH 5 minutes; stir. Cook 3 minutes more or until vegetables are crisp-tender.

4 While vegetable mixture is cooking, prepare roux. Sprinkle flour evenly over bottom of Dutch oven. Cook over high heat, without stirring, 3 to 4 minutes or until flour begins to brown. Reduce heat to medium and stir flour about 4 minutes or until evenly browned. Stir in oil until smooth. (Roux will be thick and chocolate brown.)

5 Carefully pour vegetable mixture into Dutch oven and stir until coated with roux. Stir in tomatoes and broth; bring to a boil over high heat. Reduce heat to medium; simmer, covered, 5 minutes. Serve gumbo over rice in individual bowls. *Makes 4 servings*

Prep and cook time: 30 minutes

For a special touch, sprinkle chopped parsley over each serving.

Nutrients per serving: Calories: 601, Total Fat: 33 g, Protein: 19 g, Carbohydrate: 57 g, Cholesterol: 65 mg, Sodium: 1,436 mg, Dietary Fiber: 5 g
Dietary Exchanges: Bread: 3, Meat: 2, Fat: 5

Quick Chunky Chili

1 pound ground beef
1 medium onion, chopped
1 tablespoon chili powder
1½ teaspoons ground
    cumin
2 cans (14½ ounces
    each) diced
    tomatoes, undrained
1 can (15 ounces) pinto
    beans, drained
½ cup bottled salsa
½ cup (2 ounces)
    shredded Cheddar
    cheese
3 tablespoons sour cream
4 teaspoons sliced ripe
    olives

1 Combine meat and onion in 3-quart saucepan; cook over high heat until meat is no longer pink, breaking meat apart with wooden spoon. Add chili powder and cumin; stir 1 minute or until fragrant. Add tomatoes, beans and salsa. Bring to a boil, stirring constantly. Reduce heat to low; simmer, covered, 10 minutes. Ladle into bowls. Top with cheese, sour cream and olives.

Makes 4 (1½-cup) servings

Prep and cook time: 25 minutes

Nutrients per serving: Calories: 471, Total Fat: 22 g, Protein: 34 g, Carbohydrate: 37 g, Cholesterol: 82 mg, Sodium: 1,251 mg, Dietary Fiber: 3 g

Dietary Exchanges: Vegetable: 3, Bread: 1½, Meat: 3, Fat: 2½

Serve It With Style!

To make this meal complete, just add a tossed green salad and corn bread muffins.

Pesto & Tortellini Soup

1 package (9 ounces) fresh cheese tortellini
3 cans (about 14 ounces each) chicken broth
1 jar (7 ounces) roasted red peppers, drained and slivered
¾ cup frozen green peas
3 to 4 cups fresh spinach, washed and stems removed
1 to 2 tablespoons pesto *or* ¼ cup grated Parmesan cheese

1 Cook tortellini according to package directions; drain.

2 While pasta is cooking, bring broth to a boil over high heat in covered Dutch oven. Add cooked tortellini, peppers and peas; return broth to a boil. Reduce heat to medium and simmer 1 minute.

3 Remove soup from heat; stir in spinach and pesto.
Makes 6 servings

Prep and cook time: 14 minutes

Nutrients per serving: Calories: 144, Total Fat: 4 g, Protein: 10 g, Carbohydrate: 18 g, Cholesterol: 9 mg, Sodium: 754 mg, Dietary Fiber: 2 g
Dietary Exchanges: Bread: 1, Meat: ½, Fat: 1

KITCHEN HOW-TO

To remove stems from spinach leaves, fold each leaf in half, then pull stem toward top of leaf. Discard stems.

Tuscan Vegetable Stew

2 tablespoons olive oil
2 teaspoons bottled
   minced garlic
2 packages (4 ounces
   each) sliced mixed
   exotic mushrooms *or*
   1 package (8 ounces)
   sliced button
   mushrooms
¼ cup sliced shallots or
   chopped sweet onion
1 jar (7 ounces) roasted
   red peppers
1 can (14½ ounces)
   Italian-style stewed
   tomatoes, undrained
1 can (19 ounces)
   cannellini beans,
   drained
1 bunch fresh basil*
1 tablespoon balsamic
   vinegar
   Grated Romano,
   Parmesan or Asiago
   cheese

*If fresh basil is not available, add
2 teaspoons dried basil leaves to stew with
tomatoes.*

1 Heat oil and garlic in large deep skillet over medium heat. Add mushrooms and shallots; cook 5 minutes, stirring occasionally.

2 While mushroom mixture is cooking, drain and rinse peppers; cut into 1-inch pieces. Snip tomatoes in can into small pieces with scissors.

3 Add peppers, tomatoes and beans to skillet; bring to a boil. Reduce heat to medium-low; simmer, covered, 10 minutes, stirring once.

4 While stew is simmering, cut basil leaves into thin strips to measure ¼ cup packed. Stir basil and vinegar into stew; add salt and pepper to taste. Sprinkle each serving with cheese. *Makes 4 servings*

Prep and cook time: 18 minutes

Nutrients per serving: Calories: 390, Total Fat: 9 g, Protein: 20 g, Carbohydrate: 69 g, Cholesterol: 82 mg, Sodium: 472 mg, Dietary Fiber: 14 g

Dietary Exchanges: Vegetable: 2, Bread: 4, Fat: 1½

Beer and Cheese Soup

2 to 3 (½-inch-thick)
slices pumpernickel
or rye bread
3 tablespoons cornstarch
¼ cup finely chopped
onion
1 tablespoon butter or
margarine
¾ teaspoon dried thyme
leaves
2 cloves garlic, minced
1 can (about 14 ounces)
chicken broth
1 cup beer
1½ cups (6 ounces)
shredded or diced
American cheese
1 cup (4 ounces)
shredded sharp
Cheddar cheese
½ teaspoon paprika
1 cup 2% milk

1 Preheat oven to 425°F. Cut bread into ½-inch cubes; place on baking sheet. Bake 10 to 12 minutes, stirring once, or until crisp; set aside.

2 While bread is in oven, stir 3 tablespoons water into cornstarch in small bowl; set aside. Place onion, butter, thyme and garlic in 3-quart saucepan; cook and stir over medium-high heat 3 to 4 minutes or until onion is tender. Add broth; bring to a boil. Stir in beer, cheeses and paprika. Reduce heat to low; whisk in milk and cornstarch mixture. Stir until cheese melts and soup bubbles and thickens. Ladle into bowls. Top with croutons.

Makes 6 (1-cup) servings

Prep and cook time: 20 minutes

Nutrients per serving: Calories: 296, Total Fat: 18 g, Protein: 12 g, Carbohydrate: 18 g, Cholesterol: 61 mg, Sodium: 1,111 mg, Dietary Fiber: trace

Dietary Exchanges: Bread: 1, Meat: 1½, Fat: 3

Cook's Notes

Use your favorite bottled beer to achieve the beer flavor you prefer. Bottled beer will provide a more balanced flavor than canned beer.

Szechuan Vegetable Lo Mein

- 2 cans (about 14 ounces each) vegetable or chicken broth
- 2 teaspoons bottled minced garlic
- 1 teaspoon bottled minced fresh ginger *or* ½ teaspoon ground ginger
- ¼ teaspoon red pepper flakes
- 1 package (5 ounces) uncooked Asian curly noodles or 5 ounces uncooked angel hair pasta, broken in half
- 1 package (16 ounces) frozen vegetable medley, such as broccoli, carrots, water chestnuts and red bell peppers
- 3 tablespoons soy sauce
- 1 tablespoon Asian sesame oil
- ¼ cup thinly sliced green onion tops

1 Combine broth, garlic, ginger and red pepper flakes in large deep skillet. Cover and bring to a boil over high heat.

2 Add noodles and vegetables to skillet; cover and return to a boil. Reduce heat to medium-low; simmer, uncovered, 5 to 6 minutes or until noodles and vegetables are tender, stirring occasionally.

3 Stir soy sauce and sesame oil into broth mixture; cook 3 minutes. Stir in green onions; ladle into bowls.

Makes 4 servings

Prep and cook time: 20 minutes

Note: For a heartier, protein-packed main dish, add 1 package (10½ ounces) extra-firm tofu, cut into ¾-inch pieces, to the broth mixture with the soy sauce and sesame oil.

Nutrients per serving: Calories: 274, Total Fat: 10 g, Protein: 7 g, Carbohydrate: 41 g, Cholesterol: 28 mg, Sodium: 1,517 mg, Dietary Fiber: 2 g

Dietary Exchanges: Vegetable: 2, Bread: 2, Fat: 2

LIGHTEN UP

To reduce sodium, use reduced-sodium soy sauce and reduced-sodium broth.

✦

Black and White Chili

**1 pound chicken tenders,
cut into ¾-inch
pieces**
**1 cup coarsely chopped
onion**
**1 can (15½ ounces)
Great Northern
beans, drained**
**1 can (15 ounces) black
beans, drained**
**1 can (14½ ounces)
Mexican-style
stewed tomatoes,
undrained**
**2 tablespoons Texas-style
chili powder
seasoning mix**

1 Spray large saucepan with nonstick cooking spray; heat over medium heat until hot. Add chicken and onion; cook and stir over medium to medium-high heat 5 to 8 minutes or until chicken is browned.

2 Stir remaining ingredients into saucepan; bring to a boil. Reduce heat to low; simmer, uncovered, 10 minutes.   *Makes 6 (1-cup) servings*

Prep and cook time: 30 minutes

Nutrients per serving: Calories: 268, Total Fat: 3 g, Protein: 29 g, Carbohydrate: 36 g, Cholesterol: 46 mg, Sodium: 401 mg, Dietary Fiber: 6 g

Dietary Exchanges: Vegetable: 1, Bread: 2, Meat: 2

 *Serve It With Style!*

 For a change of pace, this delicious chili is excellent served over cooked rice or pasta.

6 INGREDIENTS OR LESS

Chicken Caesar Salad

6 ounces chicken tenders
¼ cup plus 1 tablespoon Caesar salad dressing, divided
4 cups (about 5 ounces) prepared Italian salad mix (romaine and radicchio)
½ cup prepared croutons, divided
2 tablespoons grated Parmesan cheese

1 Cut chicken tenders in half lengthwise and crosswise. Heat 1 tablespoon salad dressing in large nonstick skillet over medium heat. Add chicken; cook and stir 3 to 4 minutes or until chicken is no longer pink in center. Remove chicken from skillet; sprinkle with pepper and let cool.

2 Combine salad mix, half of croutons, remaining ¼ cup salad dressing and Parmesan in serving bowl; toss to coat. Top with remaining croutons and chicken.
Makes 2 servings

Prep and cook time: 17 minutes

Nutrients per serving: Calories: 361, Total Fat: 22 g, Protein: 24 g, Carbohydrate: 13 g, Cholesterol: 57 mg, Sodium: 244 mg, Dietary Fiber: 1 g
Dietary Exchanges: Vegetable: 1, Bread: ½, Meat: 2½, Fat: 3½

Serve It With Style!

 To make this meal complete, just add a loaf of Italian bread or focaccia and for dessert, serve chocolate-dipped biscotti and fresh fruit.

Antipasto Salad Stack

8 ounces uncooked rotini pasta

2 medium tomatoes, halved lengthwise and thinly sliced

3 ounces sliced pepperoni, divided

1 can (15 ounces) red kidney beans or black beans, drained and rinsed

½ cup pimiento-stuffed green olives

¾ cup grated Parmesan cheese

1 bottle (8 ounces) Italian salad dressing

6 to 8 large romaine lettuce leaves, thinly sliced

1 Cook pasta according to package directions; drain. Cool slightly.

2 While pasta is cooking, arrange tomatoes and half of pepperoni around bottom edge of 3-quart glass serving bowl.

3 Layer cooked pasta, remaining pepperoni, beans, olives and cheese in bowl; drizzle with salad dressing.

4 Top with lettuce; cover and chill at least 1 hour or up to 24 hours.

5 To complete recipe, toss salad gently just before serving. *Makes 6 main-dish servings*

Make-ahead time: at least 1 hour or up to 24 hours before serving
Final prep time: 5 minutes

For a special touch, serve salad with peperoncini salad peppers.

Nutrients per serving: Calories: 537, Total Fat: 31 g, Protein: 20 g, Carbohydrate: 50 g, Cholesterol: 10 mg, Sodium: 1,252 mg, Dietary Fiber: 6 g
Dietary Exchanges: Vegetable: 1, Bread: 3, Meat: 1, Fat: 5½

Oriental Chicken and Spinach Salad

⅓ cup peanut oil
¼ cup honey
¼ cup soy sauce
2 teaspoons Worcestershire sauce
1 teaspoon Asian sesame oil
3 boneless chicken breast halves (about 12 ounces)
1 cup baby carrots
3 cups coarsely chopped bok choy (stems and leaves)
3 cups fresh spinach, torn into bite-size pieces
1 cup bean sprouts
¼ cup dry roasted peanuts

1 To prepare dressing, combine peanut oil, honey, soy sauce, Worcestershire sauce and sesame oil in small bowl with wire whisk until well blended.

2 Slice chicken breasts into 2 × ½-inch strips. Cut carrots crosswise into ¼-inch-thick slices. Heat 2 tablespoons dressing in large nonstick skillet over medium heat. Add chicken and carrots; cook and stir about 5 minutes or until chicken is no longer pink in center. Remove from skillet and let cool.

3 Heat another 2 tablespoons dressing in same skillet. Add bok choy; cook and stir about 1 minute or just until wilted.

4 Place spinach on individual plates. Arrange bok choy over spinach. Top with chicken, carrots and bean sprouts. Sprinkle with peanuts; serve with remaining dressing. *Makes 4 servings*

Prep and cook time: 19 minutes

Nutrients per serving: Calories: 435, Total Fat: 26 g, Protein: 25 g, Carbohydrate: 27 g, Cholesterol: 51 mg, Sodium: 1,224 mg, Dietary Fiber: 3 g
Dietary Exchanges: Vegetable: 2, Bread: 1, Meat: 2½, Fat: 4

Japanese-Style Steak with Garden Sunomono

GARDEN SUNOMONO
1 medium cucumber, peeled, seeded and thinly sliced
½ teaspoon salt
¼ cup rice wine vinegar
3 tablespoons sugar
1 cup thinly sliced radishes
½ cup julienne carrot strips

JAPANESE–STYLE STEAK
3 New York strip steaks (8 ounces each), cut ¾ inch thick
¼ cup soy sauce
3 tablespoons dry sherry
1 teaspoon Asian sesame oil
½ teaspoon ground ginger
1 large clove garlic, minced

1 To prepare Garden Sunomono, place cucumber in colander; sprinkle with salt. Let stand 20 minutes. Squeeze out liquid; rinse with water. Squeeze again.

2 Blend vinegar and sugar in medium bowl, stirring until sugar dissolves. Add cucumber, radishes and carrot. Cover; refrigerate at least 30 minutes or up to 2 hours, stirring occasionally.

3 Place steaks in shallow baking dish. Blend soy sauce, sherry, oil, ginger and garlic in small bowl; pour over steaks. Cover; refrigerate at least 30 minutes or up to 2 hours, turning steaks occasionally.

4 To complete recipe, preheat broiler. Remove steaks from marinade; place on broiler pan rack. Discard marinade. Broil 2 to 3 inches from heat 5 to 6 minutes per side or until desired doneness. Remove steaks to cutting board; slice across the grain into ½-inch slices. Serve with Garden Sunomono. *Makes 4 servings*

Make-ahead time: at least 30 minutes or up to 2 hours before serving
Final prep and cook time: 17 minutes

Serving suggestion: Serve steak with steamed jasmine or basmati rice.

Nutrients per serving: Calories: 337, Total Fat: 13 g, Protein: 39 g, Carbohydrate: 16 g, Cholesterol: 79 mg, Sodium: 701 mg, Dietary Fiber: 1 g
Dietary Exchanges: Vegetable: 3, Meat: 5

Rice and Bean Salad

1 can (about 14 ounces)
   chicken broth
2 cups uncooked instant
   brown rice
1 tablespoon olive oil
1 medium onion, chopped
3 cloves garlic, minced
2 medium carrots, cut
   into 1-inch julienne
   strips
1 medium zucchini,
   halved lengthwise
   and sliced diagonally
1 can (15½ ounces) red
   beans, drained and
   rinsed
1 can (14½ ounces)
   Italian-style stewed
   tomatoes, drained
½ cup grated Parmesan
   cheese
½ cup Italian salad
   dressing
¼ cup fresh basil leaves,
   finely chopped

1 Bring chicken broth to a boil in medium saucepan over high heat; add rice and cover. Reduce heat and cook 10 minutes or until chicken broth is absorbed. Remove from heat; set aside.

2 Heat oil in large skillet over medium-high heat. Add onion and garlic; cook and stir 2 to 3 minutes or until onion is tender. Add carrots and zucchini; cook and stir 3 to 4 minutes or until vegetables are crisp-tender. Remove from heat. Add beans, tomatoes and prepared rice; stir to combine.

3 Place rice mixture in large bowl. Cover with plastic wrap and refrigerate overnight or up to 2 days.

4 To complete recipe, add Parmesan cheese, salad dressing and basil to rice mixture; toss lightly. Season to taste with black pepper. *Makes 6 servings*

Make-ahead time: up to 2 days before serving
Final prep time: 5 minutes

Serving suggestion: Serve with flaky breadsticks or croissants and juicy chunks of watermelon.

For a special touch, garnish with tomato slices, carrot curls and a fresh basil sprig.

Nutrients per serving: Calories: 502, Total Fat: 18 g, Protein: 17 g, Carbohydrate: 74 g, Cholesterol: 13 mg, Sodium: 911 mg, Dietary Fiber: 10 g
Dietary Exchanges: Vegetable: 3, Bread: 4, Fat: 3

Chicken Stir-Fry Salad with Peanut Dressing

PEANUT DRESSING
- ½ cup chicken broth
- ½ cup smooth peanut butter
- 2 tablespoons molasses or brown sugar
- 2 tablespoons lime or lemon juice
- 1 tablespoon soy sauce
- ¼ teaspoon ground red pepper
- ⅛ teaspoon garlic powder

SALAD
- 1 pound chicken tenders, cut into ½-inch pieces
- ¼ teaspoon salt
- 2 tablespoons vegetable oil
- 1 package (16 ounces) frozen broccoli, carrots and water chestnuts blend
- 2 tablespoons soy sauce
- 1 package (10 ounces) salad greens
- ¼ cup dry roasted peanuts

1 To prepare Peanut Dressing, microwave broth on HIGH until hot, about 30 seconds. Place in blender with remaining dressing ingredients; process about 15 seconds or until well blended. Set aside.

2 Sprinkle chicken with salt. Heat oil in wok or large skillet over medium-high heat until hot. Add chicken; stir-fry 3 minutes or until chicken begins to brown.

3 Add frozen vegetables. Reduce heat to medium. Cover and cook 5 minutes more or until vegetables are crisp-tender, stirring occasionally. Stir in soy sauce. Remove from heat.

4 Arrange salad greens on plates; top with chicken mixture. Sprinkle with peanuts. Serve with Peanut Dressing.
Makes 4 servings

Prep and cook time: 20 minutes

Nutrients per serving: Calories: 521, Total Fat: 31 g, Protein: 38 g, Carbohydrate: 27 g, Cholesterol: 70 mg, Sodium: 1,322 mg, Dietary Fiber: 4 g

Dietary Exchanges: Vegetable: 2, Bread: 1, Meat: 4, Fat: 4

Garden Vegetable Pasta Salad with Bacon

12 ounces uncooked rotini or spiral pasta
½ pound bacon, thinly sliced
1 medium bunch broccoli, cut into florets
2 medium carrots, sliced diagonally
2 ribs celery, sliced diagonally
1 can (14½ ounces) pasta-ready tomatoes, drained
10 medium mushrooms, thinly sliced
½ medium red or yellow onion, thinly sliced
1 bottle (8 ounces) ranch salad dressing
½ cup (2 ounces) shredded Cheddar cheese
1 tablespoon dried parsley flakes
2 teaspoons dried basil leaves
¼ teaspoon black pepper

1 Cook pasta according to package directions. Drain and rinse well under cold water until pasta is cool.

2 Heat large skillet over medium-high heat. Add bacon; cook until browned. Remove bacon from skillet; drain on paper towels. Cool and crumble into small pieces.

3 Combine broccoli, carrots, celery, tomatoes, mushrooms and onion in large bowl. Add pasta and bacon; toss lightly. Add salad dressing, Cheddar cheese, parsley, basil and pepper; toss to combine.

Makes 6 servings

Prep and cook time: 25 minutes

Serving suggestion: Serve with sliced crusty bread.

For a special touch, top with cherry tomato slices and fresh basil sprigs.

Nutrients per serving: Calories: 511, Total Fat: 25 g, Protein: 16 g, Carbohydrate: 57 g, Cholesterol: 29 mg, Sodium: 870 mg, Dietary Fiber: 3 g
Dietary Exchanges: Vegetable: 2, Bread: 3, Meat: ½, Fat: 5

Gazebo Chicken

4 boneless chicken breast halves (about 1½ pounds)

6 cups torn Boston lettuce leaves or mixed baby greens

1 ripe cantaloupe, cut into 12 wedges and rind removed

1 large carrot, shredded

½ cup (3 ounces) fresh raspberries

⅔ cup honey-mustard salad dressing, divided

1 Preheat broiler. Place chicken, skin side down, on broiler pan rack. Season with salt and pepper to taste. Broil 4 to 5 inches from heat 8 minutes. Turn; sprinkle with salt and pepper. Broil 6 to 8 minutes or until chicken is no longer pink in center. Remove to cutting board; cool.

2 Place lettuce on large serving platter; arrange cantaloupe and carrot on lettuce.

3 Slice each chicken breast diagonally into fourths; place on lettuce.

4 Arrange raspberries on salad; drizzle with 2 tablespoons dressing. Serve with remaining dressing.

Makes 4 servings

Prep and cook time: 25 minutes

Serving suggestion: Serve salad with corn muffins and herb-flavored butter.

Nutrients per serving: Calories: 465, Total Fat: 21 g, Protein: 40 g, Carbohydrate: 29 g, Cholesterol: 103 mg, Sodium: 332 mg, Dietary Fiber: 3 g
Dietary Exchanges: Fruit: 2, Meat: 4, Fat: 2

Bacon & Potato Frittata

2 cups frozen O'Brien-style potatoes with onions and peppers
3 tablespoons butter or margarine
5 eggs
½ cup canned real bacon pieces
¼ cup half-and-half or milk
⅛ teaspoon salt
⅛ teaspoon pepper

1 Preheat broiler. Place potatoes in a microwavable medium bowl; microwave on HIGH 1 minute.

2 Melt butter in large ovenproof skillet over medium-high heat. Swirl butter up side of pan to prevent eggs from sticking. Add potatoes; cook 3 minutes, stirring occasionally.

3 Beat eggs in medium bowl. Add bacon, half-and-half, salt and pepper; mix well.

4 Pour egg mixture into skillet; reduce heat to medium. Stir gently to incorporate potatoes. Cover and cook 6 minutes or until eggs are set at edge (top will still be wet).

5 Transfer skillet to broiler. Broil 4 inches from heat about 1 to 2 minutes or until center is set and frittata is golden brown. Cut into wedges.   *Makes 4 servings*

Prep and cook time: 20 minutes

For a special touch, garnish frittata with red bell pepper strips, chopped chives and salsa.

Nutrients per serving: Calories: 332, Total Fat: 24 g, Protein: 13 g, Carbohydrate: 16 g, Cholesterol: 295 mg, Sodium: 630 mg, Dietary Fiber: 1 g
Dietary Exchanges: Bread: 1, Meat: 1½, Fat: 4

47

Salisbury Steaks with Mushroom-Wine Sauce

1 pound lean ground sirloin
¾ teaspoon garlic salt or seasoned salt
¼ teaspoon pepper
2 tablespoons butter or margarine
1 package (8 ounces) sliced button mushrooms *or* 2 packages (4 ounces each) sliced exotic mushrooms
2 tablespoons sweet vermouth or ruby port wine
1 jar (12 ounces) *or* 1 can (10½ ounces) beef gravy

1 Heat large heavy nonstick skillet over medium-high heat 3 minutes or until hot.* Meanwhile, combine ground beef, garlic salt and pepper; mix well. Shape mixture into four ¼-inch-thick oval patties.

2 Place patties in skillet as they are formed; cook 3 minutes per side or until browned. Transfer to plate; keep warm. Pour off any drippings.

3 Melt butter in skillet; add mushrooms and cook 2 minutes, stirring occasionally. Add vermouth; cook 1 minute. Add gravy; mix well.

4 Return meat to skillet; simmer uncovered over medium heat 3 minutes for medium or until desired doneness, turning meat and stirring sauce once.

Makes 4 servings

Prep and cook time: 20 minutes

If pan is not heavy, use medium heat.

For a special touch, sprinkle steaks with chopped parsley or chives.

Nutrients per serving: Calories: 341, Total Fat: 23 g, Protein: 24 g, Carbohydrate: 8 g, Cholesterol: 88 mg, Sodium: 984 mg, Dietary Fiber: 1 g
Dietary Exchanges: Vegetable: 1, Meat: 3, Fat: 3

Tempting Tuna Parmesano

2 large cloves garlic
1 package (9 ounces) refrigerated fresh angel hair pasta
¼ cup butter or margarine
1 cup whipping cream
1 cup frozen peas
¼ teaspoon salt
1 can (6 ounces) white tuna in water, drained
¼ cup grated Parmesan cheese, plus additional cheese for serving

1 Fill large deep skillet ¾ full with water. Cover and bring to a boil over high heat. Meanwhile, peel and mince garlic.

2 Add pasta to skillet; boil 1 to 2 minutes or until pasta is firm to the bite. *Do not overcook.* Drain; set aside.

3 Add butter and garlic to skillet; cook over medium-high heat until butter is melted and sizzling. Stir in cream, peas and salt; bring to a boil.

4 Break tuna into chunks and stir into skillet with ¼ cup cheese. Return pasta to skillet; cook until heated through, tossing gently with 2 wooden spoons. Serve with additional cheese and pepper to taste.

Makes 2 to 3 servings

Prep and cook time: 20 minutes

Serving suggestion: Serve with a tossed romaine lettuce and tomato salad with Italian dressing.

Nutrients per serving: Calories: 1,350, Total Fat: 75 g, Protein: 53 g, Carbohydrate: 115 g, Cholesterol: 272 mg, Sodium: 1,209 mg, Dietary Fiber: 2 g
Dietary Exchanges: Bread: 8, Meat: 4, Fat: 13

Curried Chicken, Vegetables and Couscous Skillet

1 package (16 ounces) frozen vegetable medley, such as broccoli, carrots and cauliflower or bell peppers and onions
1 pound chicken tenders
2 teaspoons curry powder, divided
¾ teaspoon garlic salt
⅛ teaspoon ground red pepper
4½ teaspoons vegetable oil
1 can (about 14 ounces) chicken broth
1 cup uncooked couscous

1 Thaw vegetables according to package directions.

2 While vegetables are thawing, place chicken in medium bowl. Sprinkle with 1 teaspoon curry powder, garlic salt and red pepper; toss to coat.

3 Heat oil in large deep skillet over medium-high heat until hot. Add chicken mixture, spreading in one layer. Cook 5 to 6 minutes or until chicken is no longer pink in center, turning occasionally.

4 Transfer chicken to plate; set aside. Add broth and remaining 1 teaspoon curry powder to skillet; bring to a boil over high heat, scraping up browned bits on bottom of skillet.

5 Stir thawed vegetables into skillet; return to a boil. Stir in couscous; top with chicken. Cover and remove from heat. Let stand 5 minutes or until liquid is absorbed.

Makes 4 servings

Prep and cook time: 19 minutes

For a special touch, add a dollop of plain yogurt to each serving.

Nutrients per serving: Calories: 402, Total Fat: 9 g, Protein: 33 g, Carbohydrate: 45 g, Cholesterol: 77 mg, Sodium: 926 mg, Dietary Fiber: 11 g
Dietary Exchanges: Vegetable: 2, Bread: 2½, Meat: 3

Speedy Beef & Bean Burritos

8 (7-inch) flour tortillas
1 pound ground beef
1 cup chopped onion
(from the salad bar or
frozen)
1 teaspoon bottled
minced garlic
1 can (15 ounces) black
beans, drained and
rinsed
1 cup spicy thick-and-
chunky salsa
2 teaspoons ground
cumin
1 bunch cilantro
2 cups (8 ounces)
shredded cojack or
Monterey Jack
cheese

1 Wrap tortillas in aluminum foil; place in oven. Turn temperature to 350°F; heat tortillas 15 minutes.

2 While tortillas are warming, prepare burrito filling. Combine meat, onion and garlic in large skillet; cook over medium-high heat until meat is no longer pink, breaking meat apart with wooden spoon. Pour off drippings.

3 Stir beans, salsa and cumin into meat mixture; reduce heat to medium. Cover and simmer 10 minutes, stirring once.

4 While filling is simmering, chop enough cilantro to measure ¼ cup. Stir into filling. Spoon filling down centers of warm tortillas; top with cheese. Roll up and serve immediately. *Makes 4 servings*

Prep and cook time: 20 minutes

Nutrients per serving: Calories: 816, Total Fat: 40 g, Protein: 47 g, Carbohydrate: 67 g, Cholesterol: 125 mg, Sodium: 1,570 mg, Dietary Fiber: 2 g
Dietary Exchanges: Vegetable: 2, Bread: 4, Meat: 4½, Fat: 5

Spicy Crabmeat Frittata

1 tablespoon olive oil
1 medium green bell
    pepper, finely
    chopped
2 cloves garlic, minced
6 eggs
1 can (6½ ounces) lump
    white crabmeat,
    drained
¼ teaspoon ground black
    pepper
¼ teaspoon salt
¼ teaspoon hot pepper
    sauce
1 large ripe plum tomato,
    seeded and finely
    chopped

1 Preheat broiler. Heat oil in 10-inch ovenproof nonstick skillet over medium-high heat. Add bell pepper and garlic to skillet; cook 3 minutes or until bell pepper is tender.

2 While bell pepper and garlic are cooking, beat eggs in medium bowl. Add crabmeat; mix to break up large pieces. Add black pepper, salt and pepper sauce; blend well. Set aside.

3 Add tomato to skillet; cook and stir 1 minute. Add egg mixture. Reduce heat to medium-low; cook about 7 minutes or until eggs begin to set around edge.

4 Transfer skillet to broiler. Broil 6 inches from heat about 2 minutes or until top of frittata is set and browned. Remove from broiler; slide frittata onto serving plate. Serve immediately. *Makes 4 servings*

Prep and cook time: 20 minutes

Serving suggestion: Serve with crusty bread, cut-up fresh vegetables and chunky guacamole.

Nutrients per serving: Calories: 202, Total Fat: 12 g, Protein: 19 g, Carbohydrate: 4 g, Cholesterol: 360 mg, Sodium: 386 mg, Dietary Fiber: trace
Dietary Exchanges: Vegetable: 1, Meat: 2½, Fat: 1

Jamaican Pork Skillet

1 tablespoon vegetable oil

4 well-trimmed center cut pork chops, cut ½ inch thick

¾ teaspoon blackened or Cajun seasoning mix

¼ teaspoon ground allspice

1 cup chunky salsa, divided

1 can (15 ounces) black beans, drained and rinsed

1 can (about 8 ounces) whole kernel corn, drained *or* 1 cup frozen whole kernel corn, thawed

1 tablespoon fresh lime juice

1 Heat oil in large deep skillet over medium-high heat until hot. Sprinkle both sides of pork chops with blackened seasoning mix and allspice; cook 2 minutes per side or until browned.

2 Pour ½ cup salsa over pork chops; reduce heat to medium. Cover and simmer about 12 minutes or until pork is no longer pink.

3 While pork chops are simmering, combine beans, corn, remaining ½ cup salsa and lime juice in medium bowl; mix well. Serve bean mixture with pork chops.
Makes 4 servings

Prep and cook time: 20 minutes

For a special touch, add chopped fresh cilantro to the bean mixture.

Nutrients per serving: Calories: 349, Total Fat: 15 g, Protein: 29 g, Carbohydrate: 33 g, Cholesterol: 65 mg, Sodium: 1,078 mg, Dietary Fiber: 9 g

Dietary Exchanges: Bread: 2, Meat: 3, Fat: 1

Serve It With Style!

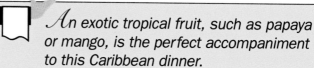

An exotic tropical fruit, such as papaya or mango, is the perfect accompaniment to this Caribbean dinner.

Ham & Barbecued Bean Skillet

1 tablespoon vegetable
   oil
1 cup chopped onion
   (from the salad bar or
   frozen)
1 teaspoon bottled
   minced garlic
1 can (15 ounces) red or
   pink kidney beans,
   drained and rinsed
1 can (15 ounces)
   cannellini or Great
   Northern beans,
   drained and rinsed
1 cup chopped green bell
   pepper
½ cup firmly packed light
   brown sugar
½ cup ketchup
2 tablespoons cider
   vinegar
2 teaspoons dry mustard
1 fully cooked smoked
   ham steak (about 12
   ounces), cut ½ inch
   thick

1 Heat oil in large deep skillet over medium-high heat until hot. Add onion and garlic; cook 3 minutes, stirring occasionally.

2 Add kidney beans, cannellini beans, bell pepper, brown sugar, ketchup, vinegar and mustard; mix well.

3 Trim fat from ham; cut into ½-inch pieces. Add ham to bean mixture; simmer over medium heat 5 minutes or until sauce thickens and mixture is heated through, stirring occasionally.   *Makes 4 servings*

Prep and cook time: 20 minutes

Nutrients per serving: Calories: 522, Total Fat: 10 g, Protein: 40 g, Carbohydrate: 85 g, Cholesterol: 47 mg, Sodium: 1,982 mg, Dietary Fiber: 16 g

Dietary Exchanges: Vegetable: 1, Bread: 4, Meat: 3, Fruit: 1

Serve It With Style!

*R*ound out this meal with a Caesar salad from a supermarket salad bar and crisp bread sticks.

Sizzling Stir-Fries

Stir-Fried Pork with Oranges and Snow Peas

1 cup uncooked rice
1 tablespoon vegetable oil
1 pound lean boneless pork, cut into ¼-inch-wide strips
½ pound snow peas, trimmed
½ cup bottled stir-fry sauce
2 tablespoons thawed frozen orange juice concentrate
1 can (11 ounces) mandarin orange sections, drained

1 Cook rice according to package directions.

2 While rice is cooking, heat oil in wok or large skillet over high heat until hot. Stir-fry pork 3 minutes or until brown and no longer pink.

3 Add snow peas; stir-fry 2 minutes or until crisp-tender. Add sauce and juice concentrate; stir until well blended. Gently stir in orange sections; heat through. Serve with rice.   *Makes 4 servings*

Prep and cook time: 20 minutes

Nutrients per serving: Calories: 419, Total Fat: 10 g, Protein: 23 g, Carbohydrate: 57 g, Cholesterol: 50 mg, Sodium: 778 mg, Dietary Fiber: 1 g
Dietary Exchanges: Vegetable: 1, Fruit: ½, Bread: 3, Meat: 2½

Chicken & Asparagus Stir-Fry

1 cup uncooked rice
2 tablespoons vegetable
    oil, divided
1 pound boneless
    skinless chicken
    breasts, cut into thin
    strips
2 medium red bell
    peppers, thinly sliced
½ pound fresh asparagus,
    cut diagonally into
    1-inch pieces
½ cup bottled stir-fry
    sauce

1 Cook rice according to package directions.

2 Heat 1 tablespoon oil in wok or large skillet over medium-high heat until hot. Stir-fry chicken 3 to 4 minutes or until chicken is no longer pink in center. Remove from wok; set aside.

3 Heat remaining 1 tablespoon oil in wok until hot. Stir-fry bell peppers and asparagus 1 minute; reduce heat to medium. Cover and cook 2 minutes or until vegetables are crisp-tender, stirring once or twice.

4 Stir in chicken and sauce; heat through. Serve with rice.

Makes 4 servings

Prep and cook time: 18 minutes

Nutrients per serving: Calories: 442, Total Fat: 11 g, Protein: 32 g, Carbohydrate: 53 g, Cholesterol: 69 mg, Sodium: 806 mg, Dietary Fiber: 3 g
Dietary Exchanges: Vegetable: 2, Bread: 3, Meat: 3

Cook's Notes

For stir-frying, select thin stalks of asparagus and cut them on the diagonal–they will cook more quickly.

Beef Teriyaki Stir-Fry

1 cup uncooked rice
1 pound beef sirloin steak, thinly sliced
½ cup teriyaki marinade, divided
2 tablespoons vegetable oil, divided
1 medium onion, halved and sliced
2 cups frozen green beans, rinsed and drained

1 Cook rice according to package directions, omitting salt.

2 While rice is cooking, combine beef and ¼ cup marinade in medium bowl; set aside.

3 While beef is marinating, heat 1½ teaspoons oil in wok or large skillet over medium-high heat until hot. Add onion; stir-fry 3 to 4 minutes or until crisp-tender. Remove from wok to medium bowl.

4 Heat 1½ teaspoons oil in wok until hot. Stir-fry beans 3 minutes or until crisp-tender and hot. Drain off excess liquid. Add beans to onion in bowl.

5 Heat remaining 1 tablespoon oil in wok until hot. Drain beef, discarding marinade. Stir-fry beef about 3 minutes or until browned. Stir in vegetables and remaining ¼ cup marinade; cook and stir 1 minute or until heated through. Serve with rice.

Makes 4 servings

Prep and cook time: 22 minutes

Nutrients per serving: Calories: 407, Total Fat: 12 g, Protein: 27 g, Carbohydrate: 46 g, Cholesterol: 65 mg, Sodium: 396 mg, Dietary Fiber: 1 g
Dietary Exchanges: Vegetable: 3, Bread: 2, Meat: 2½, Fat: 1

Sausage and Chicken Jambalaya Stir-Fry

1 cup uncooked rice
1 teaspoon vegetable oil
¼ pound chicken tenders, cut into 1-inch pieces
½ pound smoked Polish sausage, cut into bite-size pieces
1 large onion, chopped
¾ cup chopped green bell pepper
1 teaspoon bottled minced garlic
1 can (14½ ounces) diced tomatoes, drained
½ cup chicken broth
1 tablespoon dried parsley flakes
½ teaspoon dried thyme leaves
¼ teaspoon salt
¼ teaspoon black pepper
⅛ to ¼ teaspoon ground red pepper

1 Cook rice according to package directions.

2 Heat oil in wok or large skillet over medium-high heat until hot. Stir-fry chicken 2 minutes. Add sausage; stir-fry until sausage and chicken are brown, about 4 minutes. Remove from wok to medium bowl.

3 Add onion and bell pepper to wok; reduce heat to low. Cover and cook 2 to 3 minutes, stirring once or twice. Add garlic; cook and stir, uncovered, 1 minute more.

4 Add tomatoes, sausage, chicken, broth, parsley, thyme, salt, black pepper and red pepper to wok. Bring to a boil. Reduce heat to medium-low. Simmer, uncovered, 5 minutes or until most liquid has evaporated. Stir in rice; heat through.

Makes 4 servings

Prep and cook time: 30 minutes

Nutrients per serving: Calories: 464, Total Fat: 19 g, Protein: 21 g, Carbohydrate: 52 g, Cholesterol: 58 mg, Sodium: 992 mg, Dietary Fiber: 4 g
Dietary Exchanges: Vegetable: 2, Bread: 3, Meat: 1, Fat: 3

Shrimp and Vegetables with Lo Mein Noodles

2 tablespoons vegetable oil
1 pound medium shrimp, peeled
2 packages (21 ounces each) frozen lo mein stir-fry mix with sauce
¼ cup peanuts
Fresh cilantro
1 small wedge cabbage

1 Heat oil in wok or large skillet over medium-high heat until hot. Add shrimp; stir-fry 3 minutes or until shrimp are pink and opaque. Remove from wok to medium bowl. Set aside.

2 Remove sauce packet from stir-fry mix. Add frozen vegetables and noodles to wok; stir in sauce. Cover and cook 7 to 8 minutes, stirring frequently.

3 While vegetable mixture is cooking, chop peanuts and enough cilantro to measure 2 tablespoons. Shred cabbage.

4 Stir shrimp, peanuts and cilantro into vegetable mixture; heat through. Serve immediately with cabbage.
Makes 6 servings

Prep and cook time: 19 minutes

Nutrients per serving: Calories: 229, Total Fat: 11 g, Protein: 17 g, Carbohydrate: 17 g, Cholesterol: 117 mg, Sodium: 695 mg, Dietary Fiber: 1 g
Dietary Exchanges: Vegetable: 3, Meat: 2, Fat: 1

CUTTING CORNERS Since medium shrimp do not require deveining, substitute them for large shrimp whenever possible and you'll save valuable preparation time.

Spicy Tomato-Pork Stir-Fry

2 cups uncooked instant
   rice
⅔ cup tomato juice
1 tablespoon cornstarch
2 tablespoons soy sauce
¼ teaspoon paprika
3 boneless pork chops,
   cut ¾ inch thick
   (about ¾ pound)
¼ teaspoon garlic salt
⅛ teaspoon red pepper
   flakes
2 slices bacon, chopped
3 medium tomatoes,
   chopped
2 green onions, sliced
   diagonally, including
   tops

1 Prepare rice according to package directions. Set aside.

2 Combine tomato juice, cornstarch, soy sauce and paprika in small bowl, stirring until cornstarch dissolves. Set aside.

3 Slice pork across the grain into ¼-inch slices; place in medium bowl. Sprinkle pork with garlic salt and red pepper flakes; mix well.

4 Cook bacon in medium skillet over medium-high heat until brown and crisp. Remove bacon from skillet using slotted spoon; drain on paper towels. Set aside. Add pork, tomatoes and onions to skillet; stir-fry 3 minutes or until pork is barely pink in center. Stir in tomato juice mixture; cook, stirring constantly, 1 minute or until sauce thickens slightly. Remove from heat.

5 Crumble bacon; stir into pork mixture. Serve stir-fry over rice. *Makes 4 servings*

Prep and cook time: 28 minutes

Nutrients per serving: Calories: 321, Total Fat: 7 g, Protein: 15 g, Carbohydrate: 49 g, Cholesterol: 33 mg, Sodium: 875 mg, Dietary Fiber: 2 g
Dietary Exchanges: Vegetable: 1, Bread: 3, Meat: 2

Chicken with Walnuts

1 cup uncooked instant
    rice
½ cup chicken broth
¼ cup bottled Chinese
    plum sauce
2 tablespoons soy sauce
2 teaspoons cornstarch
2 tablespoons vegetable
    oil, divided
3 cups frozen bell
    peppers and onions
1 pound boneless
    skinless chicken
    breasts, cut into
    ¼-inch slices
1 clove garlic, minced
1 cup walnut halves

1 Cook rice according to package directions. Set aside.

2 Combine broth, plum sauce, soy sauce and cornstarch; set aside.

3 Heat 1 tablespoon oil in wok or large skillet over medium-high heat until hot. Add frozen bell peppers and onions; stir-fry 3 minutes or until crisp-tender. Remove vegetables from wok. Drain and discard liquid.

4 Heat remaining 1 tablespoon oil in wok until hot. Add chicken and garlic; stir-fry 3 minutes or until chicken is no longer pink in center.

5 Stir broth mixture; add to wok. Cook and stir 1 minute or until sauce thickens. Stir in vegetables and walnuts; cook 1 minute more. Serve with rice.

Makes 4 servings

Prep and cook time: 19 minutes

Nutrients per serving: Calories: 558, Total Fat: 28 g, Protein: 37 g, Carbohydrate: 43 g, Cholesterol: 70 mg, Sodium: 663 mg, Dietary Fiber: 5 g

Dietary Exchanges: Vegetable: 2, Bread: 2, Meat: 4, Fat: 3

Meat and Potato Stir-Fry

1 Heat oil in a wok or large skillet over medium-high heat until hot. Add potato, carrots and onion; cook and stir 3 minutes. Stir in broth and ½ teaspoon salt. Reduce heat to medium. Cover and cook 6 to 7 minutes more or until potato is tender, stirring once or twice. Remove vegetables from wok; set aside. Wipe out wok with paper towel.

2 Heat wok over medium-high heat until hot. Add meat and garlic; stir-fry 3 minutes or until meat is no longer pink. Add parsley, paprika, cinnamon, cumin, remaining ½ teaspoon salt and pepper; cook and stir 1 minute. Add vegetables; heat through.

Makes 4 servings

1 tablespoon vegetable oil
1 large baking potato, peeled and cut into ½-inch cubes
2 medium carrots, peeled and thinly sliced
1 medium onion, halved and sliced
⅔ cup beef broth
1 teaspoon salt, divided
1 pound lean ground round
1 large clove garlic, minced
1 tablespoon dried parsley flakes
1 teaspoon paprika
½ teaspoon ground cinnamon
½ teaspoon ground cumin
¼ teaspoon black pepper

Prep and cook time: 25 minutes

Nutrients per serving: Calories: 403, Total Fat: 19 g, Protein: 24 g, Carbohydrate: 35 g, Cholesterol: 70 mg, Sodium: 751 mg, Dietary Fiber: 4 g

Dietary Exchanges: Vegetable: 1, Bread: 2, Meat: 2½, Fat: 2

For a change of pace, serve this stir-fry as a filling for pita bread.

Barbecue Chicken with Corn Bread Topper

1½ pounds boneless skinless chicken breasts and thighs
1 can (15 ounces) red beans, drained and rinsed
1 can (8 ounces) tomato sauce
1 cup chopped green bell pepper
½ cup barbecue sauce
1 envelope (6.5 ounces) corn bread mix plus ingredients for mix

1 Cut chicken into ¾-inch cubes. Heat nonstick skillet over medium heat. Add chicken; cook and stir 5 minutes or until cooked through.

2 Combine chicken, beans, tomato sauce, bell pepper and barbecue sauce in 8-inch square microwavable ovenproof dish. Cover and refrigerate up to 2 days.

3 To complete recipe, preheat oven to 375°F. Loosely cover chicken mixture with plastic wrap or waxed paper. Microwave on MEDIUM-HIGH (70% power) 8 minutes or until heated through, stirring after 4 minutes.

4 While chicken mixture is heating, prepare corn bread mix according to package directions. Spoon batter over chicken mixture. Bake 15 to 18 minutes or until toothpick inserted in center of corn bread layer comes out clean.   *Makes 8 servings*

Make-ahead time: up to 2 days before serving
Final prep and cook time: 28 minutes

Nutrients per serving: Calories: 324, Total Fat: 8 g, Protein: 26 g, Carbohydrate: 38 g, Cholesterol: 80 mg, Sodium: 981 mg, Dietary Fiber: 3 g
Dietary Exchanges: Bread: 2, Meat: 3

Chili-Stuffed Poblano Peppers

1 pound ground beef
4 large poblano peppers
1 can (15 ounces) chili-
    seasoned beans
1 can (14½ ounces) chili-
    style chunky
    tomatoes, undrained
1 tablespoon Mexican
    (Adobo) seasoning
⅔ cup (about 2½ ounces)
    shredded Mexican
    cheese blend or
    Monterey Jack
    cheese

1 Preheat broiler. Cook ground beef in large nonstick skillet over medium-high heat 5 to 6 minutes or until no longer pink.

2 While beef is cooking, bring 2 quarts water to a boil in 3-quart saucepan. Cut peppers in half lengthwise; remove stems and seeds. Add 4 pepper halves to boiling water; cook 3 minutes or until bright green and slightly softened. Remove; drain upside down on plate. Repeat with remaining 4 halves. Set aside.

3 Add beans, tomatoes and Mexican seasoning to ground beef. Cook and stir over medium heat 5 minutes or until mixture thickens slightly.

4 Arrange peppers, cut sides up, in 13×9-inch baking dish. Divide chili mixture evenly among peppers; top with cheese. Broil 6 inches from heat 1 minute or until cheese is melted. Serve immediately.   *Makes 4 servings*

Prep and cook time: 26 minutes

Serving suggestion: Serve stuffed peppers with corn bread and chunky salsa.

Nutrients per serving: Calories: 546, Total Fat: 22 g, Protein: 40 g, Carbohydrate: 47 g, Cholesterol: 87 mg, Sodium: 1,448 mg, Dietary Fiber: 2 g
Dietary Exchanges: Vegetable: 3, Bread: 2, Meat: 3½, Fat: 2½

Four-Cheese Stuffed Shells

12 uncooked jumbo pasta shells
1 container (15 ounces) low-fat ricotta cheese
1 cup (4 ounces) shredded provolone cheese
¼ cup grated Parmesan cheese
1 egg, beaten
¼ cup chopped parsley
1 teaspoon dried basil leaves
¼ teaspoon minced dried garlic
Dash salt and black pepper
1½ cups chunky spaghetti sauce, divided
½ cup (2 ounces) shredded mozzarella cheese

1 Cook shells according to package directions, cooking only 10 to 12 minutes. Rinse, drain and set aside.

2 Combine ricotta cheese, provolone cheese, Parmesan cheese, egg, parsley, basil, garlic, salt and pepper in medium bowl. Stir until well mixed.

3 Spread ½ cup spaghetti sauce on bottom of 8-inch square glass baking dish.* Fill shells with ricotta mixture; place in prepared dish. Spread remaining 1 cup spaghetti sauce over shells. Cover tightly with plastic wrap. Refrigerate overnight.

4 To complete recipe, loosen plastic wrap from one side of dish; microwave on HIGH 5 minutes. Microwave on MEDIUM (50%) 14 to 16 minutes longer or until sauce bubbles, rotating dish halfway through cooking time. Sprinkle mozzarella cheese over top. Microwave on HIGH 1 to 2 minutes or until cheese is melted. *Makes 4 servings*

Make-ahead time: up to 1 day before serving
Final prep and cook time: 30 minutes

*To bake stuffed shells in conventional oven, preheat oven to 350°F. Bake, covered with foil, 30 minutes. Uncover and continue baking 15 to 20 minutes longer or until sauce bubbles. Sprinkle with mozzarella cheese and continue baking 1 to 2 minutes.

For a special touch, garnish with fresh basil leaves.

Nutrients per serving: Calories: 609, Total Fat: 20 g, Protein: 36 g, Carbohydrate: 69 g, Cholesterol: 89 mg, Sodium: 1,244 mg, Dietary Fiber: 0 g
Dietary Exchanges: Vegetable: 2, Bread: 4, Meat: 3, Fat: 2

Apple, Bean and Ham Casserole

1 pound boneless ham
3 cans (15 ounces each)
    Great Northern
    beans, drained and
    rinsed
1 small onion, diced
1 medium Granny Smith
    apple, diced
3 tablespoons dark
    molasses
3 tablespoons packed
    brown sugar
1 tablespoon Dijon
    mustard
1 teaspoon ground
    allspice
¼ cup thinly sliced green
    onions *or*
    1 tablespoon
    chopped fresh
    parsley

1 Preheat oven to 350°F. Cut ham into 1-inch cubes. Combine ham, beans, onion, apple, molasses, brown sugar, mustard and allspice in 3-quart casserole; mix well. Cover; bake 45 minutes or until most liquid is absorbed. Cool casserole 20 minutes. Cover and refrigerate up to 2 days.

2 To complete recipe, stir ⅓ cup water into casserole. Microwave on HIGH 10 minutes or until hot and bubbly. Sprinkle with green onions before serving.

Makes 6 servings

Make-ahead time: up to 2 days before serving
Final cook time: 15 minutes

Nutrients per serving: Calories: 411, Total Fat: 5 g, Protein: 30 g, Carbohydrate: 63 g, Cholesterol: 35 mg, Sodium: 862 mg, Dietary Fiber: 1 g

Dietary Exchanges: Bread: 4, Meat: 2

Serve It With Style!

Cut-up fresh vegetables are an excellent accompaniment for this spicy dish.

Mexican Chicken Casserole

8 ounces uncooked elbow macaroni or small shell pasta
2 teaspoons olive oil
1 large carrot, grated
1 medium green bell pepper, finely chopped
1 clove garlic, minced
¾ pound chicken tenders, cut into ¾-inch pieces
2 teaspoons cumin
1½ teaspoons dried oregano leaves
½ teaspoon salt
¼ teaspoon ground red pepper
2 cups (8 ounces) shredded Monterey Jack cheese, divided
1 bottle (16 ounces) salsa, divided

1 Cook pasta according to package directions.

2 While pasta is cooking, heat oil in large nonstick skillet over medium heat. Add carrot, bell pepper and garlic; cook and stir 3 minutes or until vegetables are tender. Add chicken. Increase heat to medium-high; cook and stir 3 to 4 minutes or until chicken is no longer pink in center. Add cumin, oregano, salt and ground red pepper; cook and stir 1 minute. Remove from heat; set aside.

3 Grease 13×9-inch microwavable dish. Drain and rinse pasta under cold running water; place in large bowl. Add chicken mixture, 1 cup cheese and 1 cup salsa. Mix well; pour into prepared dish. Top with remaining 1 cup salsa and 1 cup cheese.

4 Cover with plastic wrap; microwave on HIGH 4 to 6 minutes, turning dish halfway through cooking time. Serve immediately. *Makes 4 to 6 servings*

Prep and cook time: 20 minutes

Nutrients per serving: Calories: 591, Total Fat: 23 g, Protein: 42 g, Carbohydrate: 52 g, Cholesterol: 102 mg, Sodium: 1,443 mg, Dietary Fiber: 2 g
Dietary Exchanges: Vegetable: 1, Bread: 3, Meat: 5, Fat: 1½

Provençal Pasta Shells

12 uncooked jumbo pasta shells

1 can (6 ounces) pitted ripe olives, drained

2 tablespoons olive oil

1 teaspoon lemon juice

½ teaspoon dried thyme leaves

1½ cups (6 ounces) shredded Gruyère or mozzarella cheese, divided

⅓ cup herb-seasoned bread crumbs

1 teaspoon bottled minced garlic

1 jar (14 ounces) chunky spaghetti sauce

1 Cook pasta according to package directions; drain. Rinse with cool water; drain again.

2 While pasta is cooking, combine olives, oil, lemon juice and thyme in food processor; cover and process until puréed. Transfer to small bowl; stir in 1¼ cups cheese, bread crumbs and garlic.

3 Spread spaghetti sauce into 11×7×2-inch baking dish. Stuff each pasta shell with 2 tablespoons olive mixture. Arrange stuffed shells on sauce. Sprinkle with remaining ¼ cup cheese.

4 Cover with plastic wrap, turning back corner to vent. Microwave on HIGH 3 to 4 minutes or until cheese is melted and sauce is hot. *Makes 4 servings*

Prep and cook time: 30 minutes

For a special touch, sprinkle with chopped fresh thyme leaves.

Nutrients per serving: Calories: 650, Total Fat: 38 g, Protein: 22 g, Carbohydrate: 56 g, Cholesterol: 46 mg, Sodium: 2,172 mg, Dietary Fiber: trace

Dietary Exchanges: Vegetable: 2, Bread: 3, Meat: 1½, Fat: 6½

CUTTING CORNERS

Water will boil more quickly in a covered pan. After adding pasta to boiling water, cover the pan just until water returns to a boil.

Tamale Pie

1 pound ground beef
1 package (10 ounces)
    frozen whole kernel
    corn, thawed
1 can (14½ ounces)
    diced tomatoes,
    undrained
1 can (4 ounces) sliced
    black olives, drained
1 package (1¼ ounces)
    taco seasoning mix
1 package (6 ounces)
    corn muffin or corn
    bread mix plus
    ingredients to
    prepare mix
¼ cup (1 ounce) shredded
    Cheddar cheese
1 green onion, thinly
    sliced

1 Preheat oven to 400°F. Place meat in large skillet; cook over high heat 6 to 8 minutes or until meat is no longer pink, breaking meat apart with wooden spoon. Pour off drippings. Add corn, tomatoes, olives and seasoning mix to meat. Bring to a boil over medium-high heat, stirring constantly. Pour into deep 9-inch pie plate; smooth top with spatula.

2 Prepare corn muffin mix according to package directions. Spread evenly over meat mixture. Bake 8 to 10 minutes or until golden brown. Sprinkle with cheese and onion. Let stand 10 minutes before serving.

Makes 6 servings

Prep and cook time: 20 minutes

Serving suggestion: Serve with papaya wedges sprinkled with lime juice.

Nutrients per serving: Calories: 412, Total Fat: 20 g, Protein: 21 g, Carbohydrate: 39 g, Cholesterol: 49 mg, Sodium: 1,679 mg, Dietary Fiber: 2 g

Dietary Exchanges: Vegetable: 1, Bread: 2, Meat: 2, Fat: 3

Recipe Category Index

METRIC CONVERSION CHART

VOLUME MEASUREMENTS (dry)

⅛ teaspoon = 0.5 mL
¼ teaspoon = 1 mL
½ teaspoon = 2 mL
¾ teaspoon = 4 mL
1 teaspoon = 5 mL
1 tablespoon = 15 mL
2 tablespoons = 30 mL
¼ cup = 60 mL
⅓ cup = 75 mL
½ cup = 125 mL
⅔ cup = 150 mL
¾ cup = 175 mL
1 cup = 250 mL
2 cups = 1 pint = 500 mL
3 cups = 750 mL
4 cups = 1 quart = 1 L

VOLUME MEASUREMENTS (fluid)

1 fluid ounce (2 tablespoons) = 30 mL
4 fluid ounces (½ cup) = 125 mL
8 fluid ounces (1 cup) = 250 mL
12 fluid ounces (1½ cups) = 375 mL
16 fluid ounces (2 cups) = 500 mL

WEIGHTS (mass)

½ ounce = 15 g
1 ounce = 30 g
3 ounces = 90 g
4 ounces = 120 g
8 ounces = 225 g
10 ounces = 285 g
12 ounces = 360 g
16 ounces = 1 pound = 450 g

DIMENSIONS

1/16 inch = 2 mm
⅛ inch = 3 mm
¼ inch = 6 mm
½ inch = 1.5 cm
¾ inch = 2 cm
1 inch = 2.5 cm

OVEN TEMPERATURES

250°F = 120°C
275°F = 140°C
300°F = 150°C
325°F = 160°C
350°F = 180°C
375°F = 190°C
400°F = 200°C
425°F = 220°C
450°F = 230°C

BAKING PAN SIZES

Utensil	Size in Inches/Quarts	Metric Volume	Size in Centimeters
Baking or	8×8×2	2 L	20×20×5
Cake Pan	9×9×2	2.5 L	22×22×5
(square or	12×8×2	3 L	30×20×5
rectangular)	13×9×2	3.5 L	33×23×5
Loaf Pan	8×4×3	1.5 L	20×10×7
	9×5×3	2 L	23×13×7
Round Layer	8×1½	1.2 L	20×4
Cake Pan	9×1½	1.5 L	23×4
Pie Plate	8×1¼	750 mL	20×3
	9×1¼	1 L	23×3
Baking Dish	1 quart	1 L	—
or Casserole	1½ quart	1.5 L	—
	2 quart	2 L	—